Blah, blah, blah...

Changing your negative self-talk

Release your inner cheerleader! You deserve the best.
Barb

Barbara Small, M.A.

© Copyright 2006 Barbara Small, M.A.
All rights reserved. No part of this publication may be reproduced, stored in a retrieval system, or transmitted, in any form or by any means, electronic, mechanical, photocopying, recording, or otherwise, without the written prior permission of the author.

Note for Librarians: A cataloguing record for this book is available from Library and Archives Canada at www.collectionscanada.ca/amicus/index-e.html
ISBN 1-4251-0265-4

Printed in Victoria, BC, Canada. Printed on paper with minimum 30% recycled fibre. Trafford's print shop runs on "green energy" from solar, wind and other environmentally-friendly power sources.

Offices in Canada, USA, Ireland and UK

Book sales for North America and international:
Trafford Publishing, 6E–2333 Government St.,
Victoria, BC V8T 4P4 CANADA
phone 250 383 6864 (toll-free 1 888 232 4444)
fax 250 383 6804; email to orders@trafford.com

Book sales in Europe:
Trafford Publishing (UK) Limited, 9 Park End Street, 2nd Floor
Oxford, UK OX1 1HH UNITED KINGDOM
phone +44 (0)1865 722 113 (local rate 0845 230 9601)
facsimile +44 (0)1865 722 868; info.uk@trafford.com

Order online at:
trafford.com/06-2022

10 9 8 7 6 5 4 3 2 1

Praise for Barbara Small's first book

What About Me, What do I Want? Becoming Assertive.

"...I am learning a new way, a better way, to communicate with family, friends, and co-workers... This new way of communicating has given me an inner sense of freedom and peace I've never had before. I have found it so empowering, I've bought a book for all my friends!! I've shared tips with family members who don't even know Barb and yet in turn now say things like, "Well, doesn't it say in Barb's book?" The wisdom in this book is simple, down to earth and realistic; it makes sense, feels right and most importantly WORKS! Thank you Barb for giving me tools that I can use to make a difference in my life. What freedom!" G.S.

"Reading Barb's book was a valuable "booster shot" for me on the art and skill of assertiveness, allowing me to peel back another layer of the "onion" concerning my family of origin's communication patterns. Also the very next day I took the opportunity to set a boundary with an employer which reinforced the value of my time and work." D.G.

"This book provides "the what", "the why" and more importantly the "how to" in the pursuit of effective assertiveness. The practical tools provided, make the insightful knowledge come alive and work for me in the real world. This book is presented in a very real and honest environment which I can relate to." J. F.

Table of Contents

Introduction 1
What is self-talk? **5**
   Self-talk model 7
   Self-esteem and Self-talk 9
   Self-talk and Feelings 10
   Self-talk and Assertiveness 12
   Self-talk and Stress 13
   Self-talk and Addictions 15
   Blocking Effective Communication 17
   The Roller Coaster Response 21
How Self-talk Develops **23**
   Intention does not equal Perception 24
   How do we maintain these negative messages? 28
   Self-fulfilling Prophecy 29
   The Prevalence of Negativity 30
Common Forms of Negative Self-talk **33**
   Ten Common Cognitive Traps 34
   The World Does Not Revolve Around You 38
   It's All in the Words 41
   "The World of Should" 41
   Have to vs. Choose to 43
   I Can't 46
   But vs. And 46
   Repetition 47
   Avoid the Disclaimers 49
   Stay in the Present (the here-and-now) 50
Steps to Changing Your Self-talk **51**
   Step 1: Increasing awareness of your self-talk 52

Step 2: Whose voice is this? 54
Step 3: Challenge or dispute these beliefs or thought... 57
Step 4: Replace or reframe this belief or thought.......... 58
Step 5: Repeat this process as needed 58
Step 6: Use positive self-talk on a regular basis 60
"But I don't believe the positive statements" 60
Thought Stopping 63
Self-Dialoguing 63
It's not good, bad, right or wrong. It just is. 64
Unhelpful and Helpful Beliefs 66
Creating Positive Self-talk 69
Steps to creating positive affirmations............................ 70
Affirmations for a Healthy Self 73
Moving from new positive thoughts into action 75
Attitude is Everything... 77
Some Final Thoughts: The Power of the Positive 81
Suggested Resource List 87

Introduction

Have you ever really stopped and listened to the chatter that goes on in your head? How often have you paid attention to what you were thinking when you found yourself in an uncomfortable interaction? Did you ever wonder why two people would respond differently to the exact same situation?

We all talk to ourselves, though we might not call it that. We all have thoughts and perceptions about ourselves and the world around us. Unfortunately these thoughts and perceptions, or this self-talk, is often negative and discouraging. It can stop us from taking risks, making choices, expressing our feelings or working toward our goals. It affects the amount of stress we experience and how we behave in relationships. It interferes with our communication and determines how we interpret all situations. In short: our thoughts create our reality.

I believe that becoming aware of your self-talk is essential to making any changes in your life. I discuss the topic of self-talk and personal belief system with all my clients. I include it in every workshop; whether it is one on assertiveness skills, stress management, self-esteem, relationship or personal goal setting. I believe and have experienced that if you can change your self-talk you can change your life.

The title of this book is taken from the phrase I use when referring to my negative self-talk. I refer to it as the **"blah, blah, blah..."** that goes on in my head. I find that when it is running rampant, if I say *"yeah, yeah, blah, blah, blah..."* it helps to reduce the impact and dilute the power of my negative voice. In a sense I am letting my inner critic know that I am not willing to listen to it any more and I'm not willing to put value in what it has to say.

In the Chapter 1, I will look at what self-talk is and how it impacts our lives. I will explore the relationship between self-talk and self-esteem, stress management, addictions, assertiveness skills and communication with others.

Chapter 2 will focus on how our self-talk develops, both overtly and covertly, including how the intention of the person sending the message is not always how the other person perceives it. Next, I will discuss how we maintain negative messages even after the person who sent them is no longer in our lives, such as using self-fulfilling prophecies. I also talk about the prevalence of negativity in our society and how that contributes to us feeling more comfortable with focusing on the negative than the positive.

I will discuss the impact of this negative self-talk in Chapter 3. Changing our negative self-talk is mainly about changing the words we use when we talk to ourselves. Certain words can have a strong impact on our interpretation and perception of the world around us. I will talk about how by changing the word "should" to "could", "have to" to "choose to", and "but" to "and" we can change the focus of our thinking. Also, I will look at how repetition and the use of disclaimers can reinforce the negative impact of our self-talk. In addition, I have included a list of ten common patterns of thinking that can cause unrealistic of irrational interpretation of events.

In chapter 4, I will discuss a six-step model to help change your negative self-talk to positive self-talk. This will include increasing your awareness of your self-talk, unraveling who you learned those negative messages from, how to challenge these messages and how to replace or reframe them with positive self-talk. Chapter 5 will look at the fourth step of the model (replace or reframe this belief or thought) in more detail by looking at how to create effective positive affirmations.

Chapter 6 contains a selection of ideas to help increase the power of the positive in your life and keep your positive energy flowing strongly.

From both personal and professional experience, I believe that becoming more aware of how you speak to yourself, and recognizing the impact that this can have on your life, is essential for creating a more fulfilling and self-satisfying life. I know for sure that it has helped me to make significant changes in my own life. It is very freeing and feels so much lighter to stop overanalyzing, judging, controlling and beating myself up for everything that I am, have done, or have said. My hope is that the information contained in this book will help all of you to achieve this as well. Enjoy.

Barb

"It is only a thought and a thought can be changed. I am not limited by any past thinking. I choose my thoughts with care. I constantly have new insights and new ways of looking at my world. I am willing to change and grow." Louise Hay

What is self-talk?

"It isn't what you have, or who you are, or where you are, or what you are doing that makes you happy or unhappy. It is what you think about."
                                            Dale Carnegie

Our thoughts create our reality. They influence our feelings and perceptions about what's going on in our lives. They determine what we notice in the world around us and what we attract into our lives. By expecting the negative, we filter our experiences and interpret events in a way that meets these expectations. We see only the negative side of each situation. We pay more attention to the negative comments from others, to the decisions we made that weren't the best and to the plans that didn't work out.

Similarly, if we expect personal satisfaction, happiness and success, that is what we will attract and perceive around us. We will notice the positive opportunity that comes from losing our job or a relationship ending. We will focus on the positive feedback from our employer rather than only on the behaviours that we need to change.

Our thoughts determine how we feel, what we do, how we relate to others and all of our personal experiences. Most of these thoughts are habitual and strengthened by repeated patterns of thinking. We tend to assume they are accurate, seldom stopping to question their validity and the impact they are having on our lives. This continuous inner dialogue is called "self-talk". Our self-talk can be positive, supportive and self-enhancing or it can be negative, critical and self-defeating. The positive self-talk, we want to encourage and enhance. It is our "inner cheerleader". Our negative self-talk, our "inner critic", is the part we want to eliminate or minimize.

We talk to ourselves all day long. However, we may not always be aware of our self-talk or what we are actually saying. By neglecting to notice our negative self-talk we may be permitting a continual flow of worry and self-criticism to play in our minds and to steadily erode our self-esteem. We may also be missing out on the potential benefits of using positive self-talk to make positive changes in our lives.

Write down all the self-talk that is going through your head right now. Just use stream of consciousness and write for five minutes without editing it or judging it.

Now read it over. What is the theme or pattern that you see? Is your self-talk more positive or negative? Is there a theme running through your negative self-talk?

Self-talk model

We do not create our reality, but we do influence it by how we choose to interpret it and respond to it. We have little control over the events that happen around us and over other people's actions. What we do have control over is our response to these events. Just as we can talk ourselves into being angry, we can talk ourselves down from being angry. We can see the opportunities in a situation or we can focus on the obstacles. Our interpretation and perception of events determine the amount of stress we feel and impacts our ability to make changes in our lives.

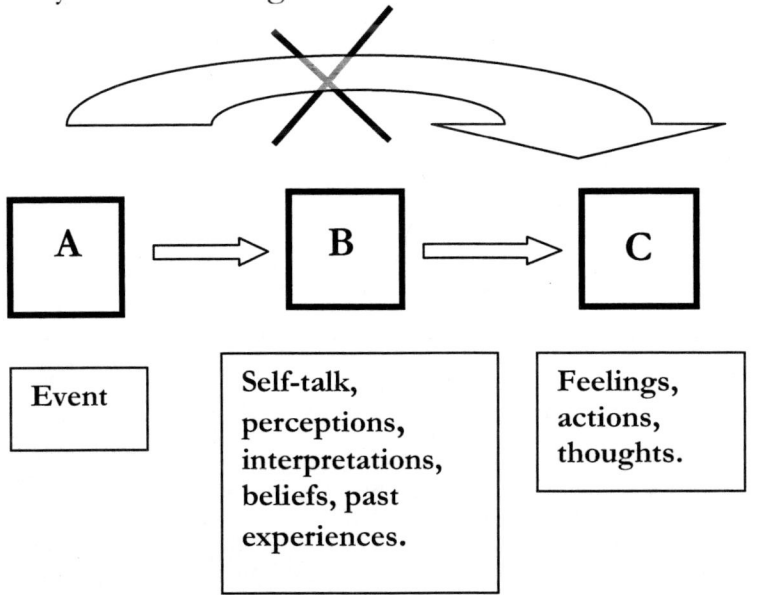

As shown in the diagram above, events (A) do not determine our feelings, actions or thoughts (C). **All events are neutral** until we place a meaning on them or interpret them based on our past experiences and our perception of the world around us. These perceptions are perpetuated by our self-talk (the "*blah, blah, blah…*" that goes on in our heads).

Our self-talk (B) determines our feelings, actions and thoughts. We do not have control over the events around us, but we do have control over our thoughts and our perceptions of these events. In the above diagram, A does not cause C; A is followed immediately by B which then determines C.

For example, one woman's husband tells her that he wants a divorce. She responds by feeling sad, hurt and disappointed. She may have said to herself that it was all her fault, that she should have tried harder and that she will probably be alone now for the rest of her life (*"blah, blah, blah…"*). A second woman's husband also tells her that he wants a divorce. She is relieved and thankful that it is over. She may have said to herself that she is glad that one of them finally took the step. Now they can get on with their lives.

The initial event is the same in each situation, but each woman's response is unique based on what she says to herself. She cannot change what her husband has decided to do, but she can change how she reacts to it.

Self-talk and Self-esteem

"Your mind can be your enemy, or it can be your friend. It can create problems or can be a tool for achieving self-esteem."
Hall and Cohn

Self-esteem and self-talk are directly related. If you have negative self-esteem you most likely have a negative tape running in your head, which is creating and reinforcing your negative self-esteem. Your "inner critic" is running the show. The longer this negative tape plays the more your self-esteem will suffer and deflate. Your negative views of yourself are reinforced each time your "inner critic" judges your actions or feelings.

If you have positive self-esteem, you are more likely saying supportive and respectful comments to yourself. You are probably more patient and flexible, and because your "inner cheerleader" is cheering you on, you continue to feel self-confident.

How do you imagine someone else would feel if you talked to him or her the way you talk to yourself? If we criticized a child in the way that many of us criticize ourselves, it would be seen as a form of abuse. Yet we will beat ourselves up and berate ourselves often on a daily basis. How we imagine that child would feel is the same way that we feel internally when we continuously talk negatively to ourselves. Besides what does beating ourselves up accomplish anyway? We usually are not more motivated as a result. Just like an abused and criticized child, our self-esteem is stripped away and we learn not to trust or believe in ourselves. We may become frozen and unable to take risks or make decisions because we are afraid of the consequences.

Self-talk and Feelings

As outlined in the self-talk model above, an event or situation does not determine the feelings we experience in response to that event. Our interpretation of it and the messages we say to ourselves determine what feelings we experience. We talk ourselves into being angry or anxious or scared. Although we may assume that anyone else would feel the same way in the same situation, it is still what we say to ourselves that determines our response. **Remember all events are neutral.**

For example, if you respond with anger to something that someone has said, it may feel like the anger happens instantaneous. But I believe that somewhere in the interaction, you have put some meaning onto what the other person has said. You have seen it as a threat or that your needs were not getting met and responded with anger. Remember if all events are neutral, then you have talked yourself into being angry. Someone else may not respond with anger in the same situation, because they have put different meaning on what was said or heard it differently. Ask yourself, "why am I angry?", "what is it about this situation that I find threatening?"

What is Self-talk?

Just as we can talk ourselves into an emotion, we can also talk ourselves out of it. We can look at the reality of the situation and our response. We can explore the payoff that this emotion has for us in this situation. Is it our way of protecting ourselves? Is it a way to avoid looking at <u>our</u> role in the situation? Is it a way to distract the other person so that we can change the subject and don't have to listen to their point of view?

Think of a situation where you responded with anger. Describe the interaction or situation. Who said what? Who did what?

Keeping in mind that <u>all events are neutral</u>, how did you talk yourself into feeling angry? What might you have said to yourself? What was the payoff for you in responding that way?

How might you talk yourself down out of your anger? Or how else might you have interpreted the situation so that you did not respond with anger?

Repeat this exercise in relation to times when you felt anxious, scared, disappointed, jealous or hurt as well.

Self-talk and Assertiveness

Our belief systems can also be an obstacle to us behaving assertively. When you develop positive beliefs about being assertive, you are more likely to engage in assertive behaviour and to continue acting assertively in the face of criticism and resistance from others. You are less likely to feel guilty after you have expressed your feelings and opinions or asked for your needs to be met.

What are your beliefs that keep you non-assertive?

- I don't have the right to be assertive
- It's selfish
- It is considered arrogant and conceited
- I will hurt the other person's feelings
- The other person will get angry
- They will take advantage of me
- I need to appear stronger than them
- Others will think I am a bitch
- Other's needs come first
- It's rude
- I will get in trouble

What are three negative beliefs you personally have about being assertive?

You can increase your ability to be assertive by replacing your non-assertive messages (self-talk) with messages that support assertive behaviour, such as, "I have the right to be assertive" or "I deserve to make choices that support me".

What are three positive beliefs that would support you being assertive? Look back at the three negative beliefs you listed above for ideas. Try changing them into positive statements.

Self-talk and Stress

Serenity Prayer
"Grant me the serenity to accept the things I cannot change. The courage to change the things I can and the wisdom to know the difference."
Reinhold Niebuhn

Have you ever wondered why some people just sail through a stressful situation while others struggle? Perhaps you know a coworker who is going through the same changes in the workplace that you are, but who is cruising through them while you are floundering.

Maybe you are focusing on everything that will be changing at work and telling yourself how you won't be able to cope with even one more change. While your smooth-sailing colleague may be perceiving the situation as something positive, as an opportunity. She may be telling herself that she can be flexible and address each challenge as it arrives. She may stay in the present and not drain her energy by trying to anticipate all that might happen. She believes in herself and knows that she can deal with whatever outcome occurs.

Our thoughts and beliefs influence the amount of stress we experience and how we handle it. It is our perception of events and what we say to ourselves that determines how stressful a situation is for us. We learn to interpret our current experiences based on our past experiences and learnings. By being aware of the meaning we place on a situation we can reduce the stress we feel through reframing our stressful thoughts into less threatening and more positive ones. Learning to replace our negative and critical self-talk with positive and self-supporting talk can change our perceptions of a situation and lead to less stress. However, some situations are real and physically threatening and need to be addressed directly.

Remember it is not the situation. It is what you say to yourself about it.

Think of a time when you felt stressed. What about that <u>particular</u> situation caused <u>you</u> to feel stressed? How did you interpret it? What did you say to yourself?

How might you have interpreted the situation differently so that you would feel less stressed? What could you say to yourself instead?

Self-talk and Addictions

I believe that negative-self-talk plays several prominent roles in addictive and compulsive behaviors. Firstly, the addictive behavior can be an effort to quiet the inner critic. Reaching for a drink, a cigarette, a quart of ice cream or compulsively shopping can all be distractions from your life and from the inner turmoil of excessive negative self-talk. The substance, or action, of choice is used to numb against uncomfortable feelings and thoughts and to shut out those critical messages that a person may carry with them. Similarly, many people with addictions find that the urge to use is often strongest when alone because that is when their negative self-talk is loudest. There are no other people or distractions to occupy their attention, so they must listen to themselves.

Secondly, negative self-talk can contribute to urges to drink, eat or use their "drug" of choice. Just as we can talk ourselves into feeling angry, scared or guilty, we can talk ourselves into "having just one more cigarette" or "I blew my diet already, so I might as well keep eating" or "really, my drinking is not a problem. I can stop any time." Our negative self-talk can be used to justify our behavior or to blame others for our unhealthy choices.

Just as negative self-talk can be used to support addictive and compulsive behaviors, positive self-talk, or our inner cheerleader, can be used to talk ourselves out of a relapse or help us not follow through with our urges to use. Positive self-talk can be effective in encouraging ourselves to make different and healthier choices. We can use it to move through our uncomfortable feelings that may be contributing to our addiction. We can counteract our persistent negative messages with positive affirmations that support us in seeing ourselves as competent, capable and worthwhile people.

Think of the last time that you used or abused your "drug" of choice, whether it be shopping, alcohol, drugs, food, cleaning, relationship, gambling or... What happened just prior to your urge to use? What were you feeling? What were you thinking or saying to yourself in your head?

How did you talk yourself in to following through with your urge? What did you say to yourself that made it okay to relapse or use? How did you convince yourself? If you didn't use, how did you talk yourself out of giving in to your urge?

Which of your patterns of negative self-talk contribute most to maintaining your addiction or compulsive behavior? How might you go about changing or reframing these statements into supportive and self-enhancing self-talk?

Blocking effective communication

Our negative self-talk also contributes greatly in determining how effective and clear our communication is with others. The self-talk creates filters that impact how we communicate and how the other person hears and interprets what we say. Our self-talk also gets in the way of us listening effectively.

Below is a diagram outlining how each person's filter can contribute to MIScommunication:

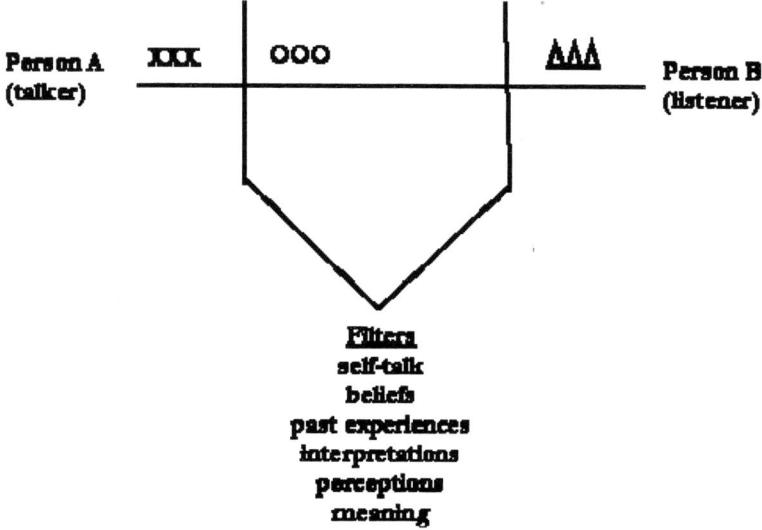

XXX = What Person A is thinking in their head that they want to say.
OOO = What actually comes out of their mouth.
∆∆∆ = What Person B hears.

Person A determines in her head what she wants to say, but what comes out of her mouth may not be what she <u>meant</u> to say. It is skewed somewhere between her mind and her mouth. It is affected by her interpretation or perception of the other person or the situation. If Person A has put a lot of importance on the interaction or is feeling nervous there is more likely to be a shift between what she thinks and what she says

What is Self-talk?

Person B interprets what Person A has said by sending it through his own filter and interpreting it based on his own self-talk, past experiences and beliefs. This can result in something totally different than what Person A intended.

The confusion is increased when Person B then responds or walks away believing that what he perceived is what Person A intended all along. Meanwhile both people leave the interaction believing that they are on the same wavelength.

For example, I had a couple in for counseling and as part of the session I had them tell each other two ways they would like their relationship to be different. Then I would have the other person repeat back what they heard their partner say.

The wife said she would like to spend more time with her friends. When asked to repeat back what he had heard his wife say, the husband quickly said, "Yeah, it's okay I heard her". I asked him to humour me and repeat back what he had heard her say. He said, "She wants a divorce!"

The husband had taken what his wife had said, "I want to spend more time with my friends" and put it through his filter and it came out the other end, as "she wants a divorce". When we explored this further the miscommunication came from their different perceptions of what marriage meant. To the husband, marriage meant that you want to spend all your free time with that person. So when his wife wanted to spend time with her friends, he assumed that she didn't want to spend time with him and therefore was not interested in being married anymore. After further discussion his filter became clearer and they were able to understand where each was coming from based on their unique self-talk, perceptions and past experiences.

Think of a conversation you had recently with someone, where you found out later that what you heard was not what he or she meant. Which of your filters contributed to this miscommunication? What do you imagine was happening for the <u>other person</u>?

Effective communication is a 2-way process. It involves talking and listening. Self-talk can interfere with being a good listener. The bottom line is that you cannot listen to two people at one time. You cannot listen to yourself and to someone else at the same time. If you are busy in your head with negative self-talk, you will not have the energy available to listen to what the other person is saying. Your self-talk may take the form of judging what the other person is saying, berating yourself in response to what the other has said or rehearsing what you plan to say. If any of these are happening, you are no longer listening to the other person.

When you realize this is happening, take a breath and focus your energy on the other person. Apologize and let them know that you missed what they just said. Ask them to please repeat it. Try not to automatically take personally what the other person is saying. Many times it has nothing to do with you and is just their opinion. Even if they are criticizing you, that is just their opinion. It does not mean that it is the only reality. You don't have to agree with them or take it on. They have the right to think it and you have the right to think differently.

The Roller Coaster Response

> There was a wise old man who was considered to be an odd sort of fellow because of the way he had of looking at things. One day, one of his favourite horses ran away, and the old man's friends rushed to console him. "That's too bad about your horse," they said. "We all feel sorry for you."
>
> "How do you know it's bad?" asked the old man. A few days later the horse returned with two beautiful wild horses following him. This brought the neighbours on the run. "Good! Good!" they exclaimed.

"How do you know it's good?" said the old man. The next day, while training the two wild horses, the man's son was thrown, and he fractured his leg. The neighbours came over to commiserate with the old man. "That's too bad about your son," they said.

"How do you know this is bad?" said the old man. The very next day a warlord and his army came through the land, conscripting able-bodied young men to fight for them. The son, of course, wasn't able to go. He had a broken leg.

Moral: It's neither good nor bad, but thinking makes it so.

Source: Unknown

How self-talk develops

We learn our self-talk, both positive and negative, by observing and listening to those around us, especially when we are young. We listen to them and make decision as to who we are, how we should act and how the world works. We hear messages both overtly and covertly.

We learn them <u>overtly</u> when we are told that we are fat, ugly or stupid. We learn them overtly when we are told that we "will never amount to anything" or that "you are just like your father". We learn them overtly when we are told, "not to trust anyone" or that "people will hurt you if you let them see your weaknesses."

We learn these messages <u>covertly</u> when we hear others talking about themselves and how they should act, look or feel. We learn them covertly when we observe our parents talking with our siblings or other family members. We learn them covertly when we see messages on TV or elsewhere in the media.

For example, we might learn to be a perfectionist by being asked directly "why did you only get 98% on an exam, why didn't you get 100%". (This is one I heard.) Or we might learn to be a perfectionist by observing our parents coming home from work and berating themselves about how they should have done better, that they didn't work hard enough.

What were some of the messages or comments that were repeated on a regular basis in your family, both positive and negative? Which ones stand out for you? Which ones do you hear coming out of your own mouth now?

Intention does not equal perception

Although we learned many of our messages and beliefs as children from our parents, have you ever wandered why your siblings or other members of your family seemed to have developed totally different perceptions or beliefs? This occurs because intention does not equal perception.

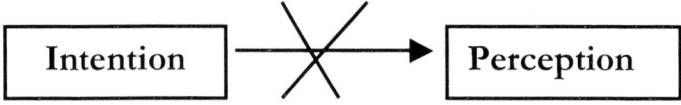

For example, a child falls and hurts himself while outside and runs inside to get comforted by mom. Mom is on the phone and does not notice him. The child could perceive this as the mom not caring and make conclusions about being hurt and looking for comfort and not getting it. He may conclude that even when he is hurt no one is there for him. He may learn messages about tears and crying and being tough. That is the child's perception, it was likely not the mom's intention, but it may be what the child walks away with and may generalize to the rest of his interactions with others.

So with this idea in mind, we now have two siblings that are being yelled at by dad. Sibling A had been yelled at by mom earlier and is still upset about that. Now when dad is yelling at her, she perceives it in a totally different way from a totally different emotional place, than her sister who was not yelled at earlier.

The message from dad is sent similarly to both daughters, yet the first child may be devastated by the discipline or comments, while the other may hardly notice it. For many people it can be simply one interaction, event or comment that can make a huge and lasting impact on them. For example, one comment about someone being fat can, when that person is in a particular state of mind, be perceived in a way that can create a negative body image or eating disorder. Or one embarrassing moment can be carried with someone for a lifetime, when others present at the same event do not even remember it happening.

An excellent example of **"*intention does not equal perception*"** comes from a client I saw regarding self-esteem and body image concerns. She told me that her mother was very negative and critical to her all the time and she felt like she could never do anything right in her mother's eyes. My client told me that she never recalls her mother ever praising her or giving her positive feedback. Over time she gathered up the courage to ask her mother why she had always been so critical and only told her everything that she did wrong. Her mother was very surprised that her daughter did not feel that she loved her and that she was hurt by her criticism.

Her mother said, "I never told you what you were doing right, because you were already doing it. But I needed to correct you on the things that you were doing wrong." Her mother's intention was to help her daughter fit in and be acceptable in society; however she focused only on what her daughter had to change and did not balance it with reinforcement for what her daughter was doing well. Meanwhile the daughter was only able to pick up the messages that her mother gave her and not read her mind regarding what she thought her daughter was already doing well.

I recall a similar situation in my own life based on my mom's response to me being teased at school because of my weight. She said that if I lost weight the other kids wouldn't tease me. Her intention was to help me avoid being teased by making me more culturally acceptable and to remove the focus of the teasing. However, what I heard was that it was okay for the other kids to tease me and that there was something wrong with me that needed to be fixed. **Intention does not equal perception.**

What are some of the negative messages that you heard in your family? These are usually some of the comments that we say to ourselves and which cause us the most problems in our lives. For example:

"No one will ever love me because I'm too fat."

"I'll never be as smart as..."

"Eventually everyone leaves you."

"I'll never have enough money. I don't want to work that hard."

"Don't get your hopes up, you'll just be disappointed."

Make a list of the most prominent negative messages that you recall. Identifying them is one of the first steps to eliminating them.

How do we maintain these negative messages?

How do we keep this negative self-talk going? How do we continue to allow it to impact our lives even after the original programmer is no longer around? Well, we do it by:

- repeating the messages to ourselves when we feel stressed, angry, anxious, hurt etc...
- regretting the past or worrying about the future
- setting unrealistic expectations for ourselves
- choosing behaviors that support these negative beliefs
- criticizing, negating and discounting ourselves
- not taking risks
- discounting our feelings
- having relationships and spending time with negative and critical people
- comparing ourselves to others
- self-criticism
- making choices that do not have integrity with our values and beliefs
- working at a job we hate or living in a home where we don't feel safe
- always putting others first

Self-fulfilling Prophecy

In addition, we create our reality based on the beliefs and self-talk in our heads. If you heard that you were just like your father and your father was an alcoholic, you might likely assume you can't do any differently and find yourself creating a lifestyle that promotes this image. Or if you are told you are not as smart as your sister, you may not bother to finish high school or even consider college or university because you believe you are not smart enough.

Have you ever heard of the term **"self-fulfilling prophecy"**? This occurs when we make choices and behave in a way that fulfills and confirms one of our negative beliefs.

For example, if I believe that every man is going to leave me, then when I get in a relationship I will probably be hyper vigilant in paying attention to my partner's behavior. I will be looking for proof that he is cheating or doesn't love me. I will look for anything that will confirm for me that he is going to abandon me.

So when he is late or looks at another woman, I will comment on it and read things into all his actions. I will accuse him of cheating or not loving me or wanting to leave me regardless of his reassurance. Eventually he may get fed up, frustrated and leave me. Then of course this confirms for me what I believed all along – "every man will leave me"!

The Prevalence of Negativity

Another reason we maintain the negative messages is because our society supports them. Negative thought is very prevalent in our society. I find that people like to commiserate and complain together. Yet, when someone focuses on the positive and talks about how wonderful their life is many people act uncomfortable. I would guess that all of you know someone who is very skilled at focusing on the negative and ensuring that we are all aware of the worse case scenario.

Research at an American University found that on the average a two-year old child hears 432 negative statements in one day. In that same 24-hour period, that child hears only 32 positive statements. That is a ratio of almost fourteen negative statements to one positive statement. Will this affect that child's self-esteem and impact what they say to themselves? Absolutely!

Let's try something...

Make a list of as many feeling words as you can come up with, such as happy, sad... Take 3-5minutes to do this. Once you have done so. Take a look at your list. How many feelings on that list would our society classify as "negative feelings" and how many would we classify as "positive feelings"?

Most people come up with a whole lot more negative feelings than they do positive ones. Sometimes we are more negative simply because that is what we are most familiar with. That is what we know the most words for.

Common Forms of Negative Self-talk

"I have suffered a great many catastrophes in my life. Most of them have never happened."
Mark Twain

If we continually say negative and critical things to ourselves, either out loud or in our heads, we continually maintain and reinforce our negative self-esteem and negative self-worth. Or if we continually place blame for the problems in our lives on external sources or on past events, we reinforce the belief that we are helpless and have no power over our own lives. It is not the specific circumstances or events which create our discomfort. It is our interpretation of those circumstances or events. We do not even have to be aware of the content of our self-talk; it can exist at a subconscious level with the same effect.

Individuals who are experiencing unhappiness, stress and problem situations in their lives often have habitual thinking patterns, which are distorted. They will often jump to conclusions without supporting evidence. Or they may react to current situations as they did to situations in the past, rather than taking time to assess the current circumstances and responding as appropriate.

Ten Common Cognitive Traps

Below is a list of Ten Common Cognitive Traps from "The Good Feeling Handbook" by Dr. David Burns. These are patterns of thinking that can cause unrealistic or irrational interpretation of events.

1. **All-or-Nothing:** You see things in black-or-white categories. If a situation is anything less than perfect, you see it as a total failure. You see only two solutions to each problem.

    "Either my marriage is perfectly happy or we might as well get a divorce."

    "Either I know my decision is absolutely correct or I don't make a decision at all."

2. **Overgeneralization:** You see a single event as a never-ending pattern of defeat by using the words "always" and "never" when you think about it.

    "I can't do anything right."

    "I'm always sitting at home alone."

"If I leave this relationship I will never find someone to love me again."

3. **Mental Filter:** You pick out a single negative detail and dwell on it exclusively. One word of criticism erases all the praise you've received. Such as, you get off the phone and all you can think of is the one thing you wish you hadn't said.

   I used to experience this when I would get evaluations back after a workshop that I had facilitated and I would focus on the one or two evaluations that were negative, rather than the many that were positive.

4. **Discounting the Positive:** You reject positive experiences by insisting they "don't count". If you do a good job, you tell yourself that anyone could have done as well.

   Many people feel quite uncomfortable when they receive a compliment. It can feel uncomfortable especially if you don't feel good about yourself or if you have been taught that it is conceited or arrogant to speak well of yourself. It can be easier to discount the compliment than to change your negative self-image. Some people may not trust the compliment, thinking the other person wants something from them.

   Our response to a compliment can often be an attempt to get the attention off us and reflect it back on to the other person. When someone gives you a compliment you just need to say, "thank you". You don't need to discount it or invalidate what they have said. Expect there to be silence, because in our society we are taught to return a compliment with minimizing ("this old thing") or redirecting it ("oh, you look great too") or discounting and focusing on the negative ("oh, but I could have done better"). When you respond this way you are negating the other person's opinion. All you need to say is "thank you". That's it. You don't have to agree with the compliment.

Open up and experience what it is like to let the positive feedback in. Be aware of your negative self-talk while you are doing so. Your self-talk can be quite informative and can help you become aware of what is blocking you from accepting compliments.

5. **Jumping to Conclusions:** You interpret things negatively when there are no facts to support your conclusion. Two common variations are "mind-reading" and "telling the future".

    "I know he won't be interested, I can just tell."

    "I'm not even going to apply for the job because I know I won't get it."

6. **Magnification and Minimization:** You exaggerate the importance of your problems and shortcomings, or you minimize your desirable qualities.

"No one else has ever had as many problems in a relationship as I've had."

"I'm not that good of an artist, anyone can paint."

7. **Emotional Reasoning:** You assume that your negative emotions reflect the way things really are.

    "All I do is cry. I am so hopeless."

    "I feel guilty. I must be a bad person".

8. **"Should" statements:** You tell yourself that things "should" be a certain way; or you "should" behave a certain way.

    "I should have tried harder."

    "I should have said I would help her move."

    I will discuss this very commonly occurring form of negative self-talk later in this chapter.

9. **Labeling:** This is an extreme form of all-or-nothing thinking. Instead of saying "*I made a mistake*", you attach a negative label to yourself: "*I'm a loser*". This cognitive trap focuses on the person rather than their behavior.

10. **Personalization and Blame:** You hold yourself responsible for events that aren't entirely under your control or you blame others for events that are only within your control.

    "I should have made him call his mother."

    "It's all his fault that I wasn't prepared for the exam."

Which ones of these Common Cognitive Traps do you experience in your life? Which are familiar? How do they impact your life?

The world does not revolve around you

Any of you who read my previous book, "*What About Me, What Do I Want? Becoming Assertive*" will recognize this section. I think the information is just as valid in the discussion of self-talk as it is in relation to assertiveness. It is our belief systems that often get in our way of being assertive and taking care of our own needs. One belief that often prevents us from expressing our true thoughts and feelings is that we are responsible for other people's feelings and for what happens in their lives. Other people are responsible for their own feelings and choices; we are not.

I thank my friend G. for a comment that became a catalyst for changing how I perceived the world. I was talking to him on the phone one day and he sounded irritated and angry. We talked for quite awhile and after I hung up, as I tended to do at that time, I obsessed about what I had said to make him angry. Then I worried that he didn't like me any more, that I had screwed up (*"blah, blah, blah…"*). I was very good at

The Impact of Negative Self-talk

continuing my conversations for hours afterward without ever involving the other person and obsessing and analyzing and, and, and…

But on this rare occasion I had the nerve to call him back. How I got the nerve I don't know. And I said to him, "You were so angry on the phone. I'm sorry. What did I say wrong?" His response was, **"The world does not revolve around you, Barb. I had a bad day at work!"**

On the outside I simply said, "Oh". On the inside, I was shocked. I thought I don't think that way. I don't think the world revolves around me. I'm always worrying about what everyone else is thinking and feeling. Worrying about whether they are all right. Worrying about whether I had offended them. But the question is, "Why do I worry about that?" So that I don't do anything to offend them. To make sure they are happy. To make sure they will still like me. So it was all about me.

I was shocked by this realization. I felt selfish. I thought I was supposed to be worried about everyone else. That if I didn't ensure they were happy, they wouldn't like me. I struggled with this insight, but it really was a catalyst for me to start taking a look at my own behaviours and choices from a different perspective.

The bottom line is that the whole world does not revolve around you, but your world does. Most people could care less about what you are doing with your life.

They are more concerned about what they are doing with their own life and whether you are looking at them or judging them.

It took me a while to figure out why this realization bothered me so much. I came to the awareness that I needed to think that others cared about what I did with my life and about me because if they didn't who would? I sure didn't at the time. I was so busy worrying about everyone else.

"The world does not revolve around you." I still remind myself of this and I share this insight with most of my clients and in almost all of my workshops. We are not as all powerful as we may think we are. Our choices and actions do not impact the <u>whole</u> world. They do impact <u>our</u> world. So when I am worried about what to say to someone. When I am over-analyzing a past conversation. When my *"blah, blah, blah…"* is running rampant. When I am making assumptions about someone else's actions or feelings and making it all about me, I remind myself, **"The world does not revolve around me."**

It's all in the words we choose

> *"Our lives are shaped not as much by our experiences, as by our expectations."*
> George Bernard Shaw

It is all about the words we choose to use. We believe what we say to ourselves. Our words create our reality. Sometimes all we have to do is change those words to start to create a new reality.

When we listen to what others say it influences us. However, we listen to ourselves far more often and for far longer than we listen to others. We have the greatest influence. Change your words. Change your thoughts. Change your life.

"The World of Should"

One of the most common forms of negative self-talk is "should" and "shouldn't". "Should" comes with shame and guilt. It reflects the rules made by the "big THEY out there". The ones who make "THE RULES".

The problem with living in the "world of should" is that it is not reality. Over here is what actually happened and you are over there in the "world of should" stuck in this downward cycle of "I should have, but I didn't, but I should have, but I didn't." And as long as you are in the "world of should" you can't problem solve the way things actually are. The reality of the situation.

Try replacing the word "should" with the word "could". Rather than "I should have accepted that job", change it to "I could have accepted that job." This leads into "I could have accepted that job and I didn't. There will be other opportunities for me in the future." Or "I could have stood up for myself, but I didn't. Next time I will say no."

"Should" implies control and rules. "Could" implies choice.

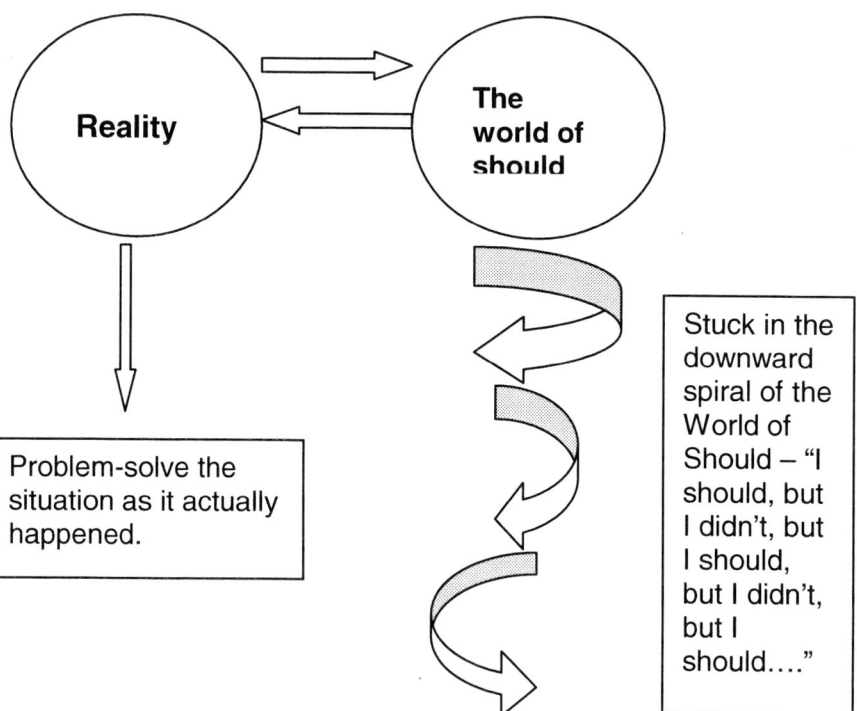

What are some of your "shoulds" that you say to yourself and that impact how you live your life? Where do you feel deficient and not good enough?

Have to vs. Choose to

The statement "have to" is similar to the word "should". It comes cloaked in the expectations of others and not from your own choice. It comes with obligation and pressure. If we don't do it, we can experience guilt and shame.

I do an activity in my self-talk workshops where I have the participants write out a list of "10 Things They <u>Have to</u> Do Every Day". They can write down anything that they feel that they HAVE TO do each day, from brushing their teeth, to going to work, to calling their mother, to feeding their kids to kissing their partner.

When everyone is finished I have each participant read their list out loud to the group and I ask them to put "I have to" in front of each of the 10 statements. *"I have to get up the morning. I have to go to work. I have to take my vitamins. I have to make the bed. I have to…"* By the time everyone in the room reads their list the energy in the room has become very low and depressing. As some people read their statements, they make comments like

"I have to do that?" They are surprised that something like kissing their partner came up on their "have to" list.

Next I have the group reread their list and put "I CHOOSE TO" in front of each of the 10 items on their list. *"I choose to get up the morning. I choose to go to work. I choose to take my vitamins. I choose to make the bed. I choose to…"* As each person rereads their list the energy in the room increases significantly. There becomes a sense of freedom and people feel like they have some control or choice in their life. They begin to look at their items and question why they are choosing to do some of these things. Many realizing that they don't really want to do the action, such as "I choose to call my mother every day." They may realize that they are doing this out of guilt and expectations on their mother's part and not because they want to.

This exercise often allows participants to begin to examine their lives, to perhaps make some changes and to start to do what they want. If nothing else, participants start to examine what it is they choose to do each day and to look at each action in a different light. This different perception is initiated simply by changing from "have to" to "choose to".

Of course there is always one or two people who question the option of putting "choose to" in front of some of their statements, because they have their *"blah, blah, blah…"* going on in their heads. They make comments, such as "but you have to brush your teeth every day" and "you have to feed your children". I help them recognize that they are doing these actions to avoid certain consequences. There are people all over the world that don't brush their teeth and unfortunately parents in the world that don't feed their children. I invite them to recognize that they personally are choosing to do these actions because they were taught to do them to avoid certain consequences, such as getting cavities in your teeth and having to go to the dentist. But it is still a personal choice.

Make a list of 10 things that you feel you <u>"have to"</u> do everyday. It can be anything from going to work, to feeding the cat, to eating breakfast. It doesn't matter what you choose.

Once you have the list of ten items read them out loud one after another with the prefix "I have to..." in front of each action. Be aware of how you feel while you are doing this.

Next repeat the process substituting the words "I choose to..." before each of the 10 activities. How does it feel when you replace the words "I have to" with "I choose to"? Are there any activities that you can't believe you are <u>choosing</u> to do? Do you want to continue to do them?

I Can't

"Can't" is only when you are physically unable to do something. Otherwise it is that you don't want to or choose not to do something.

For example if you say to me, "I can't tell my dad that I am angry with him." I could respond with "yes, you can, you are physically able to talk". What you are really saying is that <u>you don't want</u> to tell him because you are afraid of the consequences. By changing it to "I don't want to" it becomes personal and you own it.

"I can't" sounds instead like it is a written rule that everyone abides by. When you make it personal, then you recognize that this is something that you specifically learned and this gives you information into your belief system and the self-talk that is fueling your choices. Then you can directly address this obstacle and find a way to resolve it.

But vs. And

Another helpful word to eliminate from your vocabulary is the word "but". When you use the word "but" in a sentence it discounts everything in the sentence that is before it. Try replacing "but" with "and" and see how it changes the meaning of your statement.

For example, "my presentation was good, BUT I talked too fast". As soon as I say "but" what I am saying is that the presentation was not good at all, because I talked too fast. However, both can exist at the same time. I can have given a good presentation AND I could also have talked too fast. The talking too fast does not defeat the good presentation.

Or, I may say, "my husband is a loving father, BUT when he drinks he is a tyrant." This is saying that he is not a loving father because he is a tyrant when he drinks. If you change it to read, "my husband is a loving father AND when he drinks he is a tyrant". This instead says that he can be a loving father when he is not drinking and sometimes be a tyrant when he is. They can both exist at the same time.

Repetition

> *"Whatever we plant in our subconscious mind and nourish with repetition and emotion will one day become a reality"*
> Earl Nightingale

Repetition of a statement makes it real. We begin to believe it and experience it. It reinforces it in our minds. We begin to notice things in the world around us that fit with that thought or belief.

Think about when you are really tired and you walk around all day telling everyone how tired you are. "Oh, I'm so tired today. Did I tell you how tired I am? I can't believe how exhausted I am." When you finish this how do you imagine you are feeling? Probably very tired!

Be aware of some of the things that you say repeatedly to yourself throughout your day. How are you reinforcing that belief? For example, if you are unhappy in your job and everyday on the way to work you think – "Oh god, another day at this place. I can't stand it here. I can't wait for the week to be over". Your energy will likely deplete as you get nearer to work. You will probably notice every thing at the job that you hate. When co-workers talk to you they will irritate you. All this will confirm your negative thoughts of how much you hate your job.

Now if you made a conscious effort to stop this negative self-talk and to go to work with an open mind and be willing to accept that you are there until you choose to do something about it. Perhaps ask yourself, "what are some of the benefits of this particular job at this particular time in my life?" Remind yourself that you are fortunate to be employed. I believe (and have experienced) that your energy for your job will increase and you will begin to notice more and more positive aspects of your job. It may not mean that you stay in this job. It may mean, however, that your remaining days will be more satisfying.

Avoid the disclaimers

Disclaimers at the beginning of your comment or opinion, such as "maybe I am not doing this right", or "this may not be important" or ... are just your *"blah, blah, blah..."* getting in the way. It is your way of protecting yourself. In a sense you are saying – don't expect too much from me. If you like what I say then that is a bonus.

When you prefix your statements with these negative comments, it sets the stage for how others hear you and how you present yourself. It increases and emphasizes your insecurity and you will respond in a way that matches that.

When clients or students start their responses with these negative prefixes I jump in with *"blah, blah, blah..."* and ask them to start over again and just say what they want to say without the disclaimer. For some people this is going to be very difficult. They struggle with simply saying what they think. It would mean taking a risk that others may not agree, or not like what they say or that they might be making a mistake and others might judge them! When you find yourself doing this. Stop. Take a deep breath. Start again. Just say what you want to say.

What disclaimers do you tend to use? Try eliminating them from your speech for the next week. How does it feel to simply say what you think without the disclaimer in front of it?

Stay in the present (the here-and-now)

Do not worry about tomorrow, for tomorrow will worry about itself. Each day has enough trouble of its own."
Matthew 6:34.

You can't change the past and you can't control the future. Beating yourself up about things that you wished you had not done will not change them or make them go away. It just keeps your energy focused on how you screwed up.

Similarly, you can't control or predict what will happen tomorrow or the next day. We all have had the experience where we were blindsided by an event or something we would never have imagined happening. And all our best-laid plans fall apart.

Where do you spend most of your mental energy? Regretting the past? Worrying about the future? Or are you in the "moment", the "here and now"? Are you fully focused on what you're thinking, feeling and doing at this moment?

Steps to Changing Your Self-talk

"When you change the way you look at things, the things you look at change."
Wayne Dyer

In this chapter we will look at steps and techniques for decreasing your negative self-talk and increasing your positive self-talk. Outlined below are six main steps to making this change.

1. Increasing awareness of your self-talk.
2. Whose voice is this?
3. Challenge or dispute these beliefs or thoughts.
4. Replace or reframe these beliefs or thoughts.
5. Repeat this process as needed.
6. Use positive self-talk on a more regular basis.

Step 1: Increasing awareness of your self-talk

One of the first steps toward changing your negative self-talk is to become aware of it. The tape is running in our heads most of the time and influencing our choices, our emotions and our behaviors, although we may not always be aware of it. We live our lives on automatic pilot. We react to situations and circumstances, but don't know <u>why</u> we are doing so. Sometimes we do not even realize we <u>are</u> reacting. Once we are aware of our negative self-talk we can make a decision to change it.

Start by noticing the negative things you say to yourself, either out loud or in your head. You cannot change something you are not aware you are doing. Becoming aware of your negative self-talk can be one of the most difficult, yet most illuminating, aspects of this process.

Some tips to help you become more aware of your self-talk are:

1. Set specific times of the day to sit and journal. Write down everything that is going on in your head without editing it. What themes or patterns do you see?

2. Whenever you are feeling anxious, mad, sad, frustrated, or guilty, this is a time when negative self-talk is running the show. Take the time to notice what you are saying to yourself when experiencing these feelings. Write without editing

it. You may be surprised as to what you find out about yourself.

Remember all events are neutral until we put some meaning on them. We talk ourselves into being anxious. We talk ourselves into feeling angry, scared or guilty.

3. Ask a friend or family member to let you know when they hear you say negative things about yourself and put yourself down.
4. Notice when things feel incongruent in your life and consider how you are interpreting your situation that may be causing you to feel this way.

Flying on Automatic Pilot

Bring your self-talk into consciousness so that you don't run your life on automatic pilot. This is when we REACT to situations and don't know why we are reacting the way we are because it happens so fast. Our self-talk interprets and assigns meaning to an event instantaneously and as a result it is usually based solely on past experiences. We have not taken the time to assess the current situation and RESPOND based on the reality of it. For example, I meet a new person and I immediately don't like them. I don't know this new person well enough to know whether I like them or not. However, I immediately don't like them because they are male or nice to me or look like ex-best friend or.... By becoming aware of what you are saying to yourself you will be more likely to RESPOND RATHER THAN REACT in any situation.

Recall a time when you experienced a strong reaction to a new person or situation. Initially put yourself back in those circumstances. What you were thinking or saying to yourself? Write this out. Does it give you some insight as to why you reacted the way that you did?

Step 2: Whose voice is this?

Identify where your belief came from. Often it is from a comment someone said to us in the past. Whose voice have you heard say this before?

Maybe it is your mom's voice, your dad's or your grade two teacher. Who said this to you or who did you hear saying it to themselves or someone else? When you say it, whom do you sound like?

Your initial response may be to say that it is your own voice. Yes, <u>right now</u> the voice that is repeating it in your head is your own voice, but you learned it initially somewhere else. Keep in mind – **"No baby is born thinking this way"**. You learned this from someone.

By identifying where you heard this voice and whose voice it is, you can often figure out why <u>that person</u> thought that way. But ask yourself do <u>you</u> really believe this? Your dad may have thought that everyone was trying to cheat him or your grandmother may have been very worried about money because she grew up poor. But is this <u>your</u> reality now? Do <u>you</u> need to believe this too? Perhaps things have changed. Perhaps you have more resources and skills then they had.

I believe that one of the steps toward becoming an adult is to take a look at our belief systems and determine which ones are our own and which ones are someone else's that we have taken on. Which ones do we actually believe? Which beliefs have a negative impact on our life and which we want to let go of?

Write down 5 goals you would like to achieve in the next year. Now find that voice in your head that is telling you that you will never achieve these goals. We all have such a voice telling us we're too dumb, too old, too young, too fat, too whatever to do what we want. Right now, instead of telling that voice to go away, I invite you to let that voice run wild. Write for 15 minutes from the perspective of this voice and let it tell you all the reasons you will fail. Write in the second person, using the pronoun "you" (for example, "You will never reach your goals because you are so…"). Write without stopping.

There is another voice inside you. This voice knows you can succeed in doing anything you set your mind to. Everyone has this voice inside herself as well. Even you. This voice knows your strengths, your wisdom, and your creativity. Spend 15 minutes writing from this voice, telling the first voice all the reasons why you will meet your goals, and in fact probably even accomplish more during the coming year. Write in the first person, using the pronoun "I" (for example, "I know I can reach these goals because I always..."). Write without stopping. It is important to write without stopping for the 15 minutes, even if you just keep writing the same thing over and over for several minutes or write "this is silly, I don't know what to say". The longer you write the more likely you will get past the logical, socially expected and conscious reasons why and into the deeper thoughts that you are not aware of at the beginning. The real underlying thought patterns that are impacting your life.

After completing the two parts of this activity. Read the first piece of writing out loud. Who does it sound like? Your mother, your father, a sibling, a teacher, a boss? This voice is something that was taught to you. You were not born with it. Finding its origins and giving it space will help you destroy some of its power over you.

Read the second piece of writing out loud. Read it like you really mean it. Did you discover strengths you didn't know you had? Edit out self-doubts,

judgments and criticisms (they do not belong in this part of the writing exercise).

(Adapted from: SomeBody to Love, by Leslea Newman, Third Side Press, Chicago, 1991, p. 35 – 36.)

Step 3: Challenge or dispute this belief or thought

Challenge these beliefs. Dispute the reality of them. Find one example of an event, person or characteristic that does not fit this belief. Ask yourself or an impartial friend: "Is this thought accurate?", "Is it true?" Decide which of these beliefs still fit your life as it is today. Keep the ones that do, eliminate the ones that do not.

For example, if you believe that no one will love you because you are too fat. Does that mean that no one in the world who is your size or larger is in a relationship? That only thin people fall in love? Can you identify one situation that does not fit this scenario? Most likely you can and this will go toward disputing this belief.

As you do this, you will likely end up with more negative self-talk that will argue that it is different for you. Those other people found someone, but you won't. *Blah, blah, blah…*

What is your real fear about never being in a relationship? If you can't blame your weight, you may need to figure out what your true obstacle is to finding love. Perhaps it is fear. Perhaps it is that you tend to be controlling when in relationships. Perhaps… This process will allow you to identify the true obstacle as opposed to using your weight as a scapegoat. Once you identify your true obstacle you can go about dealing directly with it.

Step 4: Replace or reframe this belief or thought

Replace these negative statements with positive statements (affirmations) or reframe your self-talk with a statement, which more accurately reflects the truth. (i.e. "I have the right to express my feelings"). Repeat these positive statements whenever the negative thought surfaces. Positive affirmations can help change our attitudes and expectations about others, the world and ourselves and therefore change our perception of our reality.

See the section on "Creating Positive Self-talk" starting in the next chapter for more details on positive affirmations.

Step 5: Repeat this process as needed

As you start to replace your negative self-talk with positive self-talk, you may hear other negative self-talk disputing these positive statements. Listen to these voices and use the above steps to dispute these too.

Your self-talk will give you information on your beliefs about yourself. These will be uncovered layer by layer.

Do not repress the doubts and fears that surface when you say a positive affirmation. They are part of you and need to be integrated and accepted. Use self-dialoguing (as described in the next section) to deal with these doubts and fears or use the clearing process described next to release these negative thoughts.

Whenever you feel doubt, resistance or negative thoughts about your affirmation, take a piece of paper and write out the negative thought or the reason why the affirmation cannot work or cannot be true. Then go back to working with the affirmation.

Afterwards return to what you wrote on the paper. It will be a good indication of your negative self-talk and what is further preventing you from achieving what you want. Create an affirmation to counteract this negative thought as well and continue the process.

You may need to continue the above steps over and over again. It will take time to replace your negative self-talk and change your beliefs. Be patient and persistent. These negative beliefs were learned over time and new beliefs can also be learned. In addition, make a point of changing behaviors or choices that perpetuate the beliefs that you want to eliminate and create new behaviors and choices that support your new positive beliefs.

Step 6: Use positive self-talk on a regular basis

Start using positive self-talk whenever possible. Create your own positive reality by using positive self-talk regularly and frequently. See the next two chapters for more ideas on how to create positive affirmations and use positive self-talk to your best advantage.

Identify 3 negative statements that you say to yourself on a regular basis. For each of these statements follow through the six-step process outlined above.

How did it feel to follow these steps? What did you learn about yourself and your beliefs?

"But I don't believe the positive statements"

When I go through these steps with clients and ask them to replace their negative statements with positive ones, I always have someone say that they do not believe the positive statements when they are repeating them. They tell me that when they say them they feel embarrassed, uncomfortable, or awkward. I tell them this is normal. If you already believed them, you wouldn't need to be saying those particular affirmations. With time and repetition, the positive statements will become real and familiar. You will start to integrate them into your belief system.

We filter our world and our experiences through our belief systems. We have made meaning of our life and created a sense of self based on how we interpreted our world. When we attempt to change our self-talk and as a result our belief system, we shake up our perception of our world and ourselves. So we resist. It is easier to continue with what we have always known, rather than throw our inner world into chaos.

Once someone starts telling you how wonderful you are when throughout your life you have heard the opposite and have developed a sense of self that is negative, it is really hard to believe this incongruent message. It does not fit with your perception of self. It does not fit with how you have filtered the world and made sense of events throughout your life. It is a lot easier to discount the positive comments then to rearrange and re-categorize your whole life.

For example, if I am a bad person, then dad's negative and critical comments are because I am that bad person. If I change that perception and acknowledge that I am okay and a good person after all, how do I explain or make sense of how my dad treated me? Am I willing to acknowledge that maybe it was my dad's own issues and not about me. Maybe he really didn't know how to be a parent.

What is your fear about dreaming or thinking positive all the time? What is blocking your positive thoughts? Name it.

Also, whenever someone questions the positive statements, I point out to them that we never questioned the negative statements when they were given to us earlier in our lives. We never said, "Gee dad, why do you think I'm stupid?" Or "I don't understand why I can't trust people not to hurt me". Instead we would just absorb them, believe them and live our life based on those beliefs. Yet suddenly when someone asks us to believe that we are smart or that it is okay to make mistakes or that we deserve to be loved; we question it and doubt it.

Make a list of positive affirmations to repeat to yourself so that you feel more positive and uplifted. Place these affirmations somewhere that you can see them on a regular basis. Perhaps on your mirror, dashboard, fridge, desk or inside your closet door if you want privacy.

Thought Stopping

This is another method for relieving the continuous chatter that is in our minds. I find this especially helpful when I am trying to fall asleep at night or when I am worrying about something. It is simply a matter of saying "STOP" to yourself when you want to halt a negative thought.

It may seem too simple, but it does work. You can say it in your head or out loud. The underlying idea is that you cannot have two thoughts at one time. Your mind can only think one thought at any given time. Whatever your mind focuses on is what exists for it at that moment.

Thought stopping also works as a distracter from your negative or obsessive thought. Again it may be necessary to repeat this process several times. Follow thought stopping with reassuring and positive statements to counteract the negative ones.

Self-Dialoguing

As you dispute your self-talk and replace it with positive affirmations you may experience an increase in your self-doubt and negative beliefs. You may also experience this as you try new behaviors, be assertive or make other changes. Do not repress this information.

Instead, dialogue or hold a conversation with yourself as you would with someone else. Ask yourself what you are afraid of or what you need and then listen to yourself and what your response is. This is your inner Self trying to help you. Trust your Self and believe in what it has to say.

You know what is best for you. Your "intuition" or "gut reaction" has always been there to help you, even when you were not able or not ready to hear it. When we consistently discount our intuition and look outside of ourselves for answers or guidance, we give away our personal power to everyone else. Take back your power and take responsibility for your life and your happiness.

It's not good, bad, right or wrong. It just is.

Judging ourselves and beating ourselves up about our actions does not help us or encourage us to make changes. Actually, it can cause us to feel worse, to feel shamed and guilty. This can then paralyze us and prevent us from acting or responding to the situation.

The statement that I say to myself is *"that it's not good, bad right or wrong, it just is"*. It may not have been my best choice. Perhaps I could have done better or differently.

But the reality is that it has already happened. It is in the past and I can't change it now. So instead of beating myself up about it, I need to simply move on and decide what I need to do now to rectify the situation. This allows me to move forward rather than stay tied to the past and beat myself up.

Exploration of self-sabotage:

1. In what <u>situations</u> are you most likely to sabotage yourself?

2. Identify various <u>ways</u> you sabotage yourself:

- *What do you do/not do?*
- *What do you say to yourself at these times?*
- *Can you identify where these messages originated?*

3. How might you begin to change these patterns?

Unhelpful and Helpful Beliefs

Often people find it difficult to identify some of their negative or unhelpful beliefs and once they do, it is sometimes even harder to reframe it or replace them with something positive. Below are some suggestions that may give you some ideas. The column on the left lists some unhelpful beliefs you may have learned as a child. These can keep you from accepting yourself and asserting your rights. The column on the right lists some helpful beliefs that can challenge the unhelpful ones.

Unhelpful	Helpful
I need to be perfect	I have the right to make mistakes
I shouldn't burden others with my problems.	I have the right to ask for help and support.
I should be able to anticipate the needs of others.	Others are responsible for expressing their own needs.
When someone is in trouble, I should help them.	I need to balance my needs with the needs of others.
I should always accommodate the needs of others.	I have the right to say "no".
It is selfish to put my needs before other's needs.	I have the right to put myself first.
I should believe the views of people in positions of authority.	I have the right to my own beliefs and opinions.
I must have the approval of others to feel good about myself.	I can believe in myself and feel good without depending on others for either approval or help.

Steps to Changing Your Self-talk

I must convince others that my feelings are reasonable.	There are no "right" or "wrong" feelings, they are all valid.
I can't let myself feel angry because I am afraid I will blow up.	I can't control my feelings, but I can choose how to express them.
If I'm assertive, people won't like me.	I have the right to set my own limits and boundaries.
Things could get worse, so I shouldn't rock the boat.	I have the right to ask for what I want.

Source: Family Services of Greater Vancouver, Women's D.E.W. Program Team).

Which of these unhelpful beliefs do you recognize as being part of your negative self-talk?

When you hear them replace them with the statements from the column on the right. How does it feel when you repeat the helpful statements to yourself? What is your reaction – mentally, physically and emotionally? What does your reaction tell you?

Creating Positive Self-talk

"Most people are about as happy as they make up their minds to be."
                                                       Abraham Lincoln

An affirmation is a strong, positive statement that something is already true. Using affirmations allow us to begin to replace some of our negative self-talk with more positive and self-encouraging self-talk. Affirmations can help change our attitudes and expectations about others, the world and ourselves and thereby change our perception of our reality. Affirmations can be said silently, spoken out loud or written out. They can be any positive statement.

The theory behind affirmations is that you are accepting what currently exists in your life, while at the same time creating new positive opportunities for what you would like in your life. Research shows that our brains do not know the difference between imagination and reality.

Similar electrodes fire when imagining or visualizing a situation as when actually experiencing it.

Steps to creating positive affirmations

1. Create the affirmation in the **present tense** (" I am...", "I have..."). Treat it as if it already exists. Research has found that self-talk used in the first-person and in the present tense has the fastest impact on the development of new beliefs. Identify your need/want and state it as if you already possess it.

    If you create the affirmation in the future tense, such as saying "I will..." it is very easy to put it off and not follow through. Your brain hears it as "maybe one day, but not now".

2. State the affirmation in the **positive**. ("I am assertive with others" rather than "I do not let others discount my needs"). State what you <u>do</u> want, not what you don't want.

    It is believed that your brain does not hear the "do not". What it hears is "I let others discount my needs". This also allows you to focus your energy in the direction you want to move, rather than focusing on what you are trying to stop.

3. **Repeat** them daily. The more you repeat the positive affirmations, the more power they will have. There are various techniques to help reinforce positive self-

talk. The impact is greatest if more than one technique is used simultaneously.

- Spend time each day reading the positive statements out loud
- Reinforce them by writing the positive affirmations in a journal or notebook
- Place the statements on cards or post-its and put them where you'll see them often
- Listen to positive affirmations recorded onto cassettes
- Snap your finger after saying them to cement them in place by involving all modalities – visual, auditory and tactile.

4. Don't worry if in the beginning you don't believe the affirmations. If you did believe them you would not need an affirmation for that area of your life. Also, just as our unquestioned negative beliefs became self-fulfilling prophecies in our life, by repeating positive statements we can create a positive reality for ourselves.

5. Affirmations work best when you are **relaxed** and in an open state of mind. Focus on <u>accepting</u> rather than forcing them.

6. The **shorter and simpler** the affirmation the more effective it will be. Often when we make them too long we tend to contradict ourselves or they become confusing.

7. Do not repress the doubts and fears that surface when you say an affirmation. They are part of you and need to be integrated and accepted. Use self-dialoguing to deal with these as outlined in the previous chapter or use the clearing process described next to release the negative thoughts.

Whenever you feel doubt, resistance or negative thoughts about your affirmation, take a piece of paper and write out the negative thought or the reason why the affirmation cannot work or cannot be true. Then go back to the affirmation. Afterwards return to what you wrote on the paper. It will be a good indication of your negative self-talk and what is preventing you from achieving what you want in your life. Create an affirmation to counteract this negative thought as well.

Write out the habitual things you say to yourself. Change the negative statements to positive ones. Write out the positive ones 10 times each.

If negative thoughts come up then flip that paper over and write out the negative thoughts and then go back to the positive ones. Later you can go back to the new negative messages and repeat this process to replace them as well.

Every day and in every way you are getting better and better.

I remember a student in one of the employment skills courses that I taught at the local college. He stood out from the other students because of his confidence and the self-assurance that he portrayed. When we were doing the module on self-talk as a class, he shared that while he was growing up, every night when his parents put him to bed they said to him, "every day and in every way, you are getting better and better". He still remembers that and it has helped him to feel good about himself throughout his life. The impact of this positive affirmation was very clear to me in his actions and choices. For me this was a vivid example of the power of the positive.

Affirmations for a Healthy Self

Below are some examples of some positive affirmations. Read these statements every day until they become part of your thinking.

1. I am a unique and precious human being; always doing the best I can, always growing in wisdom and love.

2. I am in charge of my own life.

3. My number one responsibility is my own growth and well being. The better I am to me, the better I will be to others.

4. I refuse to be put down by the attitudes or opinions of others.

5. I make my own decisions and assume the responsibility for any mistake; however, I refuse to feel shame or guilt about them.

6. I am not my actions; I am the actor. My actions may be good or bad; but that does not make me good or bad.

7. I am not free as to the things that will happen to me. But I am 100% free as to the attitude I have toward these things. My personal well-being or my suffering depends on my attitude.

8. I do not have to prove myself to anyone. I need only express myself as honestly and effectively as I am capable.

9. I am free of animosity or resentment.

10. My emotional well being is dependent primarily on how I love me.

11. I am kind and gentle toward me.

12. I live a day at a time, do first things first.

13. I am patient and serene for I have the rest of my life in which to grow.

14. Every experience I have in life, even the unpleasant ones, contributes to my learning and growth.

15. No one in the world is more important than I as a person.

16. My mistakes and non-successes do not make me a louse, a crumb or whatever. They only prove that I am imperfect, that is, human. And there is nothing wrong with being human.

Source unknown.

Moving from new positive thoughts into action

The power of self-talk is in how it can affect your behavior. By examining your self-talk you can change actions that are self-defeating. To experience the power of your positive self-talk you need to ensure that your behavior is congruent with it.

Reframing or replacing your negative self-talk with positive is only an initial step. The next challenge is to maintain that positive self-talk and to make different choices and act differently in your life as a result of your new positive thoughts. Remember your thoughts create your reality.

One way to make this change is to ensure that your actions are congruent with your new thoughts. If you have decided to no longer be a perfectionist and have decided that it is okay to make mistakes, then you need to step away from your computer when you are reading over your report for the fourth time or follow through with a decision when you are not 100% sure that it is the correct decision.

Examine your behavior by asking yourself the following questions:

- *What behavior has my negative self-talk created in my life?*
- *How has it hindered me?*
- *What actions would be congruent with my new positive self-talk?*
- *How will my life be improved if I follow through with behaviors that match my new positive self-talk?*

Heart Cards

Mario Biasio, a counsellor and author in Victoria, BC, has created a wonderful resource called them "Heart Cards – 72 messages to lighten your journey". Each of

Creating Positive Self-talk

these inspirational cards contains a positive statement such as, *"your success can be truly amazing now", "go for the best", "allow more love into your life"* or *"be grateful for what you have and more will come"*.

I find them very encouraging and uplifting. I will choose one each morning or during the day when I am feeling negative. I also like to pass them around at the end of a workshop so that each participant can take away a positive thought. Many stores in Victoria, BC sell Heart Cards or you can visit www.heart.ca for more information on how to purchase your own set.

Attitude is Everything

Jerry is the kind of guy you love to hate. He is always in a good mood and always has something positive to say. When someone would ask him how he was doing, he would reply, "If I were any better, I would be twins"! He was a natural motivator. If an employee was having a bad day, Jerry was there telling the employee how to look on the positive side of the situation. Seeing this style really made me curious, so one day I went up to Jerry and asked him, "I don't get it! You can't be a positive person all of the time. How do you do it?"

Jerry replied, "Each morning I wake up and say to myself, you have two choices today. You can choose to be in a good mood or you can choose to be in a bad mood. I choose to be in a good mood. Each time something bad happens, I can choose to be a victim or...I can choose to learn from it. I choose to learn from it. Every time someone comes to me complaining, I can choose to accept their complaining or I can point out the positive side of life. I choose the positive side of life."

"Yeah, right, it's not that easy," I protested.

"Yes, it is," Jerry said. "Life is all about choices. When you cut away all the junk, every situation is a choice. You choose how you react to situations. You choose how people affect your mood. You choose to be in a good mood or bad mood. The bottom line: It's your choice how you live your life."

I reflected on what Jerry said. Choices! Soon thereafter, I left the restaurant industry to start my own business. We lost touch, but I often thought about him when I made a choice about life instead of reacting to it. Several years later, I heard that Jerry did something you are never supposed to do in the restaurant business. He left the back door open one morning and was held up at gunpoint by three armed robbers. While trying to open the safe, his hand shaking from nervousness, slipped off the combination. The robbers panicked and shot him. Luckily, Jerry was found relatively quickly and rushed to the local trauma centre. After 18 hours of surgery and weeks of intensive care, Jerry was released from the hospital with fragments of the bullets still in his body.

Creating Positive Self-talk

I saw Jerry about six months after the accident. When I asked him how he was, he replied, "If I were any better, I'd be twins. Wanna see my scars?"

I declined to see his wounds, but I did ask him what had gone through his mind as the accident took place.

The first thing that went through my mind was that I should have locked the back door," Jerry replied. "Then, as I lay on the ground, I remembered that I had two choices: I could choose to live or I could choose to die. I chose to live."

"Weren't you scared? Did you lose consciousness?" I asked.

Jerry continued, "...the paramedics were great. They kept telling me I was going to be fine. But when they wheeled me into the ER and I saw the expressions on the faces of the doctors and nurses, I got really scared. In their eyes, I read he's a dead man. "I knew I needed to take action."

"What did you do?" I asked. "Well, there was a big burly nurse shouting questions at me," said Jerry "She asked if I was allergic to anything. Yes, I replied. The doctors and nurses stopped working as they waited for my reply. I took a deep breath and yelled, "Bullets."

Over their laughter, I told them, "I am choosing to live. Operate on me as if I am alive, not dead." Jerry lived, thanks to the skill of his doctors, but also because of his amazing attitude... I learned from him that every day we have the choice to live fully. Attitude, after all, is everything.

(Source: Brian Cavanaugh from A Cup of Chicken Soup for the Soul.)

Some Final Thoughts: The Power of the Positive

"Energy follows thought; we move toward, but not beyond, what we can imagine. What we assume, expect, or believe creates and colours our experience. By expanding our deepest beliefs about what is possible, we change our experience of life."
Dan Millman

This chapter contains a selection of ideas to help increase the power of the positive in your life and keep your positive energy flowing.

1. Remember that your thoughts create your destiny. Recognize your own power to create your life.

2. Stop worrying. "Worrying about a problem is like trying to do calculus by chewing bubble gum". (Baz Luhrman)

3. Don't believe in defeat. "There are no failures, just different outcomes." (Anthony Robbins) If you turn around you may notice unexpected opportunities. Also, when you feel defeated, make a list of the factors that are for you, rather than focusing on those that are against you.

4. Stop the little negatives because they grow in to large ones.

5. Fill your life with positive and supportive people.

6. Name what is blocking your positive thoughts. What prevents you from thinking positive all the time?

7. Examine each of your core beliefs in terms of how it operates in your life. Make a commitment to yourself to eliminate the ones that cause you distress or problems.

8. Focus on the present. Your energy is drained by regretting the past and worrying about the future. Stay grounded in the here-and-now where it is easier to actually problem-solve the real situations.

9. When faced with a problem, focus on possible solutions and the resources that you do have. Brainstorm. What are the many options available, not just the black-and-white solutions or obvious ones?

10. Take self-responsibility. Stop blaming others for your unhappiness. Recognize the results of your

choices. "The key to you is always within you." (Wayne. Dyer)

11. Identify your personal definition of success. This helps you decide which path you want to take and to know when you have arrived at your goal. Your definition of success will be unique to you. No one else can define it for you.

12. Fill your life with positive supportive people. Allow their positive opinion of you in. Try not to block them because their opinions do not fit your image of yourself. What is the worse thing that could happen if you thought positive thoughts about yourself? You might actually feel more energetic and motivated and have more fun!

13. Avoid draining your energy by focusing on the past and looking at mistakes that have already been made. Focus on the lesson learned and not on the mistake. What can you learn from the choice you made, whether it was a good choice or not?

14. Express your appreciation and positive feelings toward others. Say thank you when they complete simple daily tasks. Avoid draining your energy focusing on what they didn't or haven't done.

15. When feeling overwhelmed by change, make a list of what is staying the same and what is not changing. What do you already know? What can you keep doing the same as before?

16. Acknowledge out loud your positive traits and successes. Question why it is considered conceited or arrogant to talk about what you do well.

17. Keep a gratitude journal. Each night before bed list three things that you are grateful for that day. Some days it may simply be that you are grateful that the day is finally over!

18. Work at being content with who you are rather than pleasing others by wearing your social mask. When you wear a mask and try to be everything to everyone it can be exhausting. There is no space left for you. Also, I find that in order to please everyone I would have to keep switching masks for each new person because everyone will want something different. *"You died the day you lived for someone else."* (Source unknown).

19. Ask yourself: "How do I manufacture my own unhappiness?"

20. Keep asking yourself what is really important. In five years how much will this really matter?

21. Brainstorm a list of what makes you happy. Direct your attention to what pleases you. How can you allow or create more of this in your life?

22. Practice random acts of kindness.

23. Suspend judgment of yourself and others. Practice self-acceptance and acceptance of others. What does judging yourself or someone else achieve? Acceptance does not mean never changing.

However, you cannot change what you don't recognize or accept you are doing.

24. Affirm and reaffirm your assets. List ten achievements you have obtained over the last 5 years. It could be finding a new job, taking a course, learning a new skill or changing your attitude.

25. Trust your intuition. Your intuition is that "gut feeling" or that hunch. It is your inner self speaking to you.

26. Create a home environment that is pleasing and nurturing to you.

27. Work at a job that energizes you.

28. Slow down. Learn to respond, rather than react.

29. Our own attitude is often what we see reflected in others. People in our lives often act as mirrors to allow us to see ourselves more clearly.

    If you are surrounded by negative people, take a look at yourself. How might these people be a reflection of your own attitude?

    Similarly, as you become more positive you will attract more positive people to you. Initially though, as you become more positive the negative people in your life may escalate their negatively in order to try to pull you back in. Remember it is not your job to change them. Focus your energy on being more positive and creating more positive energy in your <u>own</u> life.

Which 5 of these suggestions will you commit to focusing on over the next 6 months?

Suggested Resource List

Briggs, Dorothy. (1977). Celebrate Your Self: Enhancing Your Own Self-Esteem. New York: Doubleday & Company Inc.

Burns, David. (1989). The Good Feeling Handbook. New York: William Morrow & Co., Inc.

Carlson, Richard. Don't Sweat the Small Stuff..... and it's all small stuff.

Carson, Richard. (1995). Taming Your Gremlin. New York: Harper Collins.

Davis, Martha, Elizabeth Eschelman & Matthew McKay. (1988). The Relaxation & Stress Reduction Workbook (3rd Edition). CA: New Harbinger Publications.

Gawain, Shatki. (1985). Creative Visualization. New York: Bantam Books.

Goulding, Mary and Goulding, Robert. <u>Not to Worry!: How to Free Yourself from Unnecessary Anxiety and Channel Your Worries into Positive Action.</u>

Hall, Lindsey & Leigh Cohn. (1990). <u>Self-Esteem: Tools for Recovery</u>. CA: Gurze Books

Hay, Louise. (1984). <u>You Can Heal Your Life</u>. CA: Hay House.

King, Serge. (1981). <u>Imagineering for Health</u>. Illinois: Theosophical Publishing House.

Levine, Barbara. (1991). <u>Your Body Believes Every Word You Say</u>. CA: Aslan Publishing.

Peale, Norman Vincent. <u>The Power of Positive Thinking.</u>

Russianoff, Penelope. (1988). <u>When am I Going to be Happy: How to Break the Emotional Bad Habits that Make you Miserable</u>. New York: Bantam Books.

Video

LaRoche, Loretta. <u>Joy of Stress.</u>

About the author:

Barbara Small has a Bachelor's degree in Psychology and a Master's degree in Counselling. She has been working with clients in private practice for over a decade. Barb facilitates workshops for the general public, businesses and community agencies on various topics, including assertiveness skill, self-esteem, self-talk, communication skills and managing change. Barb lives and works in Victoria, BC. Her first book, *"What About Me, What Do I Want? Becoming Assertive* was released in September 2005.

Additional copies of either of Barb's books can be purchased from the author. Contact Barb at:

Tel: (250) 384-9020
Fax: (250) 384-9024
Email: barbsmall@shaw.ca
www.barbsmallcounselling-coaching.com

ISBN 1425102654